All of It

poems by

Kat Crawford

Finishing Line Press
Georgetown, Kentucky

All of It

Copyright © 2021 by Kat Crawford
ISBN 978-1-64662-592-5 First Edition
All rights reserved under International and Pan-American Copyright Conventions. No part of this book may be reproduced in any manner whatsoever without written permission from the publisher, except in the case of brief quotations embodied in critical articles and reviews.

ACKNOWLEDGMENTS

"It's All in the Details" previously titled "From the Ground Up" in *Tuxedo* at Dominican University

On the way to this book there has been a veritable troupe of visionaries, leaders, angels and fellow pilgrims. Writers, professors of poetry, parents, children and dear friends have all joined in to shepherd and strengthen me. Their voices and their light taught me to keep going and to keep saying my truth.

My deepest thanks go to my precious husband, Gregg and our creative and spirited children, Whitney and Ben. They are all in the "band." My appreciation, respect and extreme gratitude for the entire "village" are, honestly, far too great for this page. I hope that at least by naming them here, I can begin to honor them. Their creativity, intelligence and hard work brighten the way for me constantly.

With a deep bow, I thank my teachers, mentors and fellow poets, Margaret Kaufman, Joan Baranow, Judy Halebsky, the Band of Poets (Catharine Clark-Sayles, Brennen Belagorsky, Bogie Bougas, Rob Hotchkiss, Kathy Chance and Allison Baldwin), Prartho Sereno, Galway Kinnell, David St. John, Rick Benjamin, Diane O"Keefe, Terry Lucas and last but certainly not least, Finishing Line Press who opened the door for me!

Publisher: Leah Huete de Maines
Editor: Christen Kincaid
Cover Art and Design: Alida Morgan
Author Photo: John Andrew Murphy

Order online: www.finishinglinepress.com
also available on amazon.com

Author inquiries and mail orders:
Finishing Line Press
PO Box 1626
Georgetown, Kentucky 40324
USA

Table of Contents

All of It	1
Neighborhood	3
Ode to Flags	4
The Plumeria Tree	5
It's All in the Details	6
Ode to Rising	7
It Would Be Odd	8
Ode to My Daughter's Hands	10
Now You See It	13
Ode to Broken and Lost Things	14
In The Endless Night	15
Ode to Flotsam and Jetsam	16
Dream before the Concert	17
Ode to Good Things	18
Ode to the Children	19
Hualalai Road	20
Ode to Wasted Time	21
The Words In Between	23
The Salvation of Words	24
…Something's Happening Here	25
Guts	26
What She Left Behind	27
Ode to the Labyrinth	28
Aubade	29
A Different America	30

All of It

Where it comes from and how it moves
in hearts, memory, is a mystery—vital elements.
Everything counts—trees, nests, red-tailed hawks
dandelions that close at night, telephone wires
cell towers painted to look like trees
curling bark, dreams, laundry on clothes lines,
ripe apricots, Broadway tunes, sea spray,
peonies, reminders of every moment ever.

A great flood of the world and its contents.

Food vendors on street corners, New York,
mushrooms, aloe vera, foreign films
trips, lips painted in Russian Red, dangly earrings
Matisse, mountains of books, your team
winning the World Series, breathing, watching
a lover breathe, grace of rain, trains, forgiveness.
Where they come from and how they finally reach
their destination is not up to us.

A great flood in the world and its contents.

In this season of green, storms or welcome wind,
Others make surprise appearances, a black cat
on a noodle shop roof, geckos in a house,
an argument that fizzles, a shy voice speaking up,
progress made in anything, a toddler who says
thank you my darling, losing the match and laughing,
a changed mind, remembering a joke, carrying
unbearable weight because someone said you could.

A great flood of acceptance in the world and its contents.

How each one made it here might be of interest but too much study spoils the sheen, glisten, prickle and shiver of it all.
Stay close, say something. *Don't try, don't act.*
It is all too magnificent to manipulate.
It is all too crazy to change. Can you stay for a while?
Get close to it? Skin on skin. Nostrils flared.
Ecstasy from the center. Let loose with the right touch the resonant voice we choose.

Neighborhood

Shall the names be changed? I throw windows open, light on odd human grandeur.

Start right on the corner, Miss Broadhead brown plaid, gap-toothed. Just to utter her name awakens her soul. May be a witch—run! Never saw her with groceries. *What did she eat?*

Around the corner Dr. O'Keefe cut off my ring, ruby and bent, constricting blood flow. His dental tools' glint in kitchen light. Mrs. stood close, small crucifix on her sweater set. Where were the pictures of Jesus?

We scratched chalk numbers in squares, hopscotch. Mr. Thompson's. The tallest house.
His flesh finery from my window, fresh from his bath. Elevator, no kids, scent of old wood, cigars, African safaris. Who was his lover?

Pavlows' next, pristine and sleek—beautiful mother, father, no one touch *anyone. Please whatever you do, do not step on the white rug.* I see you in your window. Perfection
no affection. No dogs no cats. They'll all come back one day, for more.

Longing for touch, Mrs. Monteagle's bisque hands. Divine, cypress trees pointy thrones to parrots—wild & green. Curves, caws, exotic tails,
claws clung to trellis & branch to gaze upon her. They knew where to feed.

Never venture to the next door—in gold late afternoon, Mrs. Alexander,
invisible, in and out, petite, tanned. Lumbering father, often away. Billy, wild-eyed son, risky, blustery buck in a T-Bird, in lust, look quick or you'll miss him.

Keep soul secrets, spill truth of their missions, handed to them from deathbeds, bibles and dreams.

Ode to Flags

there is good in any spangled light, two sailboats, mirrors
gold beacons for seekers—Morning papers arrive

refrain we've heard before. I turn to crows, pines—
old with a wink of hope. Bold and bright

I pledge allegiance with a smothered heart.
Flags anyone might follow stars, stripes, sheaves of wheat

How will we make new names for flags? Name them for the women,
for the men, the ones who dug, built, wept and bled.

Never fold them. Raise them with their faces.
All that is needed are gusts of unbridled wind.

The Plumeria Tree

Come, walk under my branches
smile at my blossoms heavy with nectar.
Dead ones, edges curled and brown, grass
still wet from night.
Gather fragrance in your linen shirt
string them together in leis
Inhale my scent
lie down under me for as long as I am here.
Your tears feed my roots.

It's All in the Details

Gilded from the flannel of hours, paws pad down paths,
small tongues lap from moss green ponds with the ingenuity of
morning.

Flower to flower activity, precision of bees, dewfall, answers to dream
questions.

Is this escape? What we used to take for granted. When the pink
cheek of sunset slips into blue dusk and white-hot stars clinch the
deal—we get it.

He looks, she looks, squinting to understand, light has made its way
in, moon almost full (like when you say *ooh look, the moon
is full tonight*. Someone says *no, not quite*). As if a night or two before
or after makes a difference.

It does. Everything counts for something. Owls' hoot, dry leaves
underfoot, whistle for the dog, songs in school, bravery, sky
in early evening, *any sky.*

Ode to Rising

On red linoleum it stands: Magic Chef
polished majesty, handles, heat, ready, open
for risen holy communion in tin pans,
egg-wash crust, perfect crumb & perfume
inviting as zinnias, sweet peas rise
offer up their pink to the fine morning,
hummingbirds sip in carmine carnations.

In our slippers & robes, we pad down
outside wooden stairs, honeysuckle air, peer in,
breathe in bread, jam, juice. Reliable. Board and flour,
deft. Knead and turn, heels of hands. Strong arms
from loaves and loaves. Every orange tree gave
too much juice. Hundreds spill
onto the orchard floor.

We ran up and down the rows. Baskets
swinging, waning moon, hot sun
with Ah-mama and Aha love came easy.
Sissy and I in our fiesta regalia, hibiscus queens
danced & snapped fingers, small casteñets
ay, ay, ay of mariachis, we freed ourselves,
fearless, waved away cares.

Burning sun multiplied days, full hearts
bore fragrant nights. Everything grew—
jasmine, morning glories, crickets, cows.
Ah-mama and *Aha* echoed every call
eagles and seagulls, dolphins, blue whales
dressed in barnacle finery,
only a sailboat journey away.

It Would Be Odd

if I didn't recall the weather on November 13th
the day mom died or would it? I just know
we ran outside to find my sister's runaway dogs.

Curled on a way too narrow hospital bed—love circle.
Me   Mom   my sister.
Deep cancer plaques & tangles. Morticians wheeled mom's body
burgundy velvet bag, gurney glint over sidewalk squares.
Coach of a hearse—dry gutter—once a river for walnut shell boats.
Felt the sun as we ran down a neighbor's driveway. Maggie nowhere
to be found, ran from death. On my way I dashed my name on
strange papers I'd never seen, death certificates—where ashes would
go.
Years later flew into star jasmine and Kua Bay.

The nurses, (as mom preferred to call them, not caregivers) gave
chase til we came upon the pup yelping in a culvert. *Pehrfect*
proclaimed the Irish nurse, *your mum is definitely here with this dog
drama*-her brogue made her A's flat. Perfect. People say that all the
time to make things good and fine. Rough edge of loss made soft in
seconds. A wooden ladder appeared. I shimmied down in the sliver
of a pit to lift the panicked dog. Descended and pushed her up and
out. Alleluia! Then more postmortem tasks ahead.

Mary, one childhood friend of Mom's, planned her own funeral.
Everything. Her clothes, music, even her daughter's floral suit.
Casket with rose satin lining. What do they do before a cremation?
How do they treat the body? What do they remove?
Was there more than one person there?
Did they know her kindness? Maybe we should have been there.
In India the body is washed and wrapped by the family before they
send the funeral pyre down the Ganges River. Holy water. She used to
say *I want to go home.* Where is her holy river?
How *does* the soul travel? Is death dark for the dying?

Her gray-blue eyes searched for home. Moline, pretty name for a town. Soft like heaven.

Ode to My Daughter's Hands

the very smallness of them,
snipped tawny curls
then hid them behind her bed,
she gave me knowledge to hold, put, preen, pat
to center, to paint what I saw
as the blue of her eyes
somewhere close to ours.
Hands cupped in a softball mitt
hard to catch, trained eye to hand
their slender shape led me to her
gifts of wit, melodic laughter,
giant love heart, songs
shells & color beyond the pale,
lace scarves, fur scraps, full skirts, silver sandals,
hailed us down from a great highway
over here she would say,
hands waving, smiling
Cut paper, cotton ball trees,
dolls, fair like her, stitch along lines,
wrote her name everywhere,
trim the tree with Y's and W's
they ting when struck
Gold girl, you bring us round full circle
to what you know & it rings true
that single note.

Stolen Memory

With great draughts from bedside water,
thirsty as I've been, I uncurl from night,
on wooden floors to pray once more, plain words
turn into air—should there be more

with cool water I splash myself awake
over eyes and lips that spoke just hours before
through dreams and black halls cursing the present
with eyes of the past, strange and pure lens

to see things newly, rest from the dank din
sit on a cushion, three sticks of incense
send up hope, as if amber and patchouli air, silence
might quell some angry god

who is really there who knows who might hear
watch as vetiver ashes fall red-crested cardinals' trill
peck for seeds, worms all the grass bounty that sates
their hunger. Soft smoke journeys to a grand cerulean sea

this soft symphonic hum constant ring in the ether
tingsha a low roar of feral voices cats bullfrogs owls
any creature near a love bazaar where every soul sings & circles
calling us to join the choir beat the drum

with great wing-like swinging of arms descend onto taut rawhide
made from skin of our animal ancestors
strange booming to carry us through the dark
to the ecstasy of a clearing where light points pierce

like a needle with silver thread. It splays warp & woof
spreads them just enough to enter to weave a shimmer
slender tail in and out donning the indigo cotton
with just enough light to catch the eye of the beholder

then, these incantations, with a warm fire
a woman carrying water a song before the meal
or a name faded from my mind disappeared
in the dusty lavender distance keep ringing brass bells

calendar the planting check the weather dig
so seeds receive tilled beds & flourish
when sun dirt and water feed and ripen furrows
string up the little fence around them. Lay the bird netting and wait.

Now You See It

now, you don't.
I said to my kid sister as I snitched
what was hers. Didn't matter.
I was older. Dolls, diaries,
skate keys, 45's. Affection & care
raked over coals,
ashes. Dry stick words,
great stacks, cut branches,
dead blooms, no leaves,
no arcing stems
no longer lithe banners on trees.
In their original state
before summer they were new
pale with fur—like a baby.

What pulls me away
from pristine beauty to wildfire fear,
foul fuel poured over
quiet's unsuspecting splendor?
Anyone in its path
their shadow cast in flames' light.
Massive fires scourge our inner lands
fine hearts & handmade souls
too young to burn
too young to self-destruct
Had I planted grass and some Irish moss
this might be a different story.
Go to the garden I tell myself. Get on your knees
turn soil with bare hands to see.

Ode to Broken and Lost Things

A tortoiseshell button, wooden shards from a Chinese lamp
suede shoes with a missing heel, an old car with a muffler dragging
lost cell phones, a wooden fence, collapsed barns,
glasses, socks without mates, voices grown soft, bones,
teeth and nails, chipped & rusted sinks, pearl necklaces,
door latches—we try to save some of them hoping
the story of the shoes, the button, the lamp or the voice is not over
yet. Tsunami of cities, shouts, fear, ruckus of roughness take over,
pushing everything in its path aside. Ballast of people,
deep roots, wild love every second. Forgiveness.
Strange counterpoint to the rampage.

Great numbers of trees and people turn towards a light.
Is chaos the call that's needed?

Endless Night

rocking back and forth
you asleep without a twitch, Turning,
dim memory of pale nightclothes
softer than the sting of nightmares
darting in and out. Fearless calm
came up my body from a crackling sky
lit up, split my tree-body
divided by my branches
legs, arms, breasts, blades. Two braids,
two sides. What is the straight story?
Don't worry. —If I should die before I wake—
Right brain tells left to keep reaching.
Lucid tales of journeys of mad hares and fairies.
Just keep your baby blues closed on everything
even steady breathing now.
I did not know brilliant green of Illinois grass, brazen crickets.
Catapult to this—midnight morass asking *which way darlin'*
what are you dreamin' to fix, fixin' to dream?
You could have it all in a garden
in this overstuffed life, water it.
Poems, courage, pears, apple blossoms,
climbers onto giant walls of the castle
that I found in a book of someone else's dreams.
Walk, breathe until you rest
in some semblance of a garden where leaves
turn their backs on an incoming storm.

Ode to Flotsam and Jetsam

Waves of it across desks and in dressers
trapped by scaly corners, under unsuspecting sheets
blankets, where perhaps a lowly dead bedbug
has breathed its last breath suffocated by an eiderdown cover.
Bedside table drawers the grand stations where trains of the stuff
of a life appear—no passengers except the owners, of earplugs
hotel pens, chargers, bookmarks & vital night creams.
All of it jostles for a place of importance. Back and forth
over papers and notes they slide day in and day out. Clean it
and you will never find the damn thing again. Broken parts of lamps,
dead batteries sidle onto counters. Theatre tickets,
cards too dear to toss, stack themselves cozy in more drawers
or worse, on shelves. There were bags, yes, bags of rsvp cards
(when people used to send them) and carefully paper-rationed
Christmas cards in my mother's saved papers—friends for a party—
why on earth would anyone throw them out? Staid and responsible
those cards. Legos, doll clothes and glasses all to make things
happy, kind. Now they float around houses like shadows
looking for their source. Formed and yet, unformed,
as they have lost their creator like us, looking for ours.

Dream before the Concert
> *Lose your dreams and you might lose your mind.* —Mick Jagger

Someone shot at a deer and missed—both bullets entered my arm
made two holes, the fleshy part under muscle. Missed the mark.

Everyday events; a London kiosk, a rosy ticket woman, our change for
 the tickets,
not missing a beat. Rolling Stones hot sex rockers, Mick's tongue,
hungry eyes, mic-humping, juice harps.
Red cape gold high tops skintight jeans wa-wa

nights together sheets sweat steeped vibrations of '63, king of all of it
peace sign, crowns over the dead returning from 'Nam, eyes closed.

I slow my breath to ask the question. All of us in this.
Ice melts sun beats we run from each other light candles draw
water from wells.

Where is the divining rod?

Ode to Good Things

A small café table with Belgian waffles
surrounded by a group of friends
paper-thin petals of wildflowers
scruff of feathers on a raven's head
salty skin after swimming
slicing glassy water
hug of fog
apricot dusk
deep kissing
talking when there is time
curved arc of a sail
stridency of wet eucalyptus
currents' curl on water
a stroller with twins
dogs that know the sound of toast
a chair for an unexpected guest
red lipstick on shapely lips
quiet of a library
holding hands with a grandparent
soft skin, tuberose and narcissus perfume
planting tomatoes
music anywhere
orange trees in blossom
people raising a roof
breaking in a new baseball glove
lighting candles
bathing my young children
knowing family stories
waking from a good dream
delivering happy news
a mind opening
knowing what is right
not having the answer
rest, grace.

Ode to the Children

Every car sprouts wings to rise
above the blush blue clouds. Disappear.
adults vanish. Mockingbirds & eagles
flutter and dive, hover over willows, fragrant pines.
Woodpeckers tap primal rhythms.
Wild horses slow to let the youngest jump
on their glossy backs. Corn tassels adorn their manes.
Sun adds her glow and all manner of insects strut to drums
crawl towards their homemade huts and mounds.
Every color vermillion, saffron, moss and sea
vibrates as if new; just born. Chestnuts, pinecones
walnuts fall, waiting. Children craft tiny boats,
elfin figurines, fairies. The older ones braid maiden grass
while symphonic waves play; majestic songs
from caw, caw, kwa-wee, keeeeeeeeer
calling them to join in.
It's safe, it's safe! Come out, come out!
Waves of laughter make rites of spring.
exotic beasts emerge growling low,
soft purring, trumpeting as welcome
for the young. Unleashed hearts,
brains with drawings of dragons,
close their eyes to artifice
guiding sight to bright finery of fields,
losing themselves in secret languages.
Mysterious words *Ishti mudalis, sedders and bochaneaters*—
we thought we knew everything.

*nicknames for types of people created by the poet's family friend (an adult)

Hualalai Road

I was the last one
fumbling with directions
yearning for sunset in lilac light
without my satellite guide my car lurched forward
even though our church friend warned us
the ancestors know
the church was built over them
carpenters and priests bless the land
before they hammer one nail
small flies buzzed over us
as we told life stories
scripture & young promises
circled blue walls protecting us
as we prayed to the Designer of everything
dark roads, mesquite trees, saffron flowers,
headlights, mongoose, feral cats, painters,
healers, thieves, teachers and drunks.
infinitesimal parts we play
everyone reveals clues to the next brushstroke
even thorns on the mesquite tree
one piercing may not be enough.

Instead of a left turn on Queen's Highway
I curve up the hill—wind around
high on a carved road, Mamalahoa
my eyes glance toward the sea
headlights snake in patterns then
on a curve of the road from black bushes
a wild pig huge in heft & hair made me brake
to know, the plans we make are just the start.

Ode to Wasted Time

What did you think
beloveds of the world
counting all the days
wall calendar wildflowers
photos every month
apricot sun, spun silver moon
reach for you,
silence deafens tired eyes.
You persisted
with dream knowledge
to open your famished mind
hands awaken
for your joy-partner
torn pages fall like dry leaves
til every thought & word
you said I said all rest
in the Great Subconscious
they go nowhere
except when called
late in indigo nights,
cool grey of days,
to pray to greet to rant
of too many people
cars, even flies on hot days.
Time flies you repeat monthly
where does it go we ask
needing God or *anyone*
to paint elegant replies
long beaches appear
verdant parks grow up
festooned in cypress & shells
familiar music adorns quiet
that might go unnoticed.
Imperceptible growth takes place
green caterpillar fuzz
tiny hairs we cannot see

until the butterfly is caught
stunner's gold and black spots
in small hands
knows warmth
but we barely noticed
with coffee, toast, cherry jam
or was it honey
& the soft body beside you?

Will the trickle of minutes
ever stand still while you cry and moan
and right before you
rises the great golden alarm
radiant outside your window?
Does the mundane
have its way with you?
Tidy drawers.
Pay for light and gas.
Brush hair.
What happens to us
what keeps giving us chills
in this giant wave
that we might just miss
talking fast, looking down
over and over
refrains of truth
songs, art & firelight
hints of sight
are where and when they all matter.

The Words in Between

it could be a place in Botswana
simple words that morph on the page from overuse
or the quick clicks from a nimble tongue
new language that makes you stop, take a breath.
Ask how that works you say, *say it again*
just so I can understand & he does, just to get
a feel for the space between you, your world and his
sweet, wild air traveling through bulrushes
shimmer of space on top of water, around a boat,
before the rising hippopotamus grand and deep,
submerged with eyes on the edge of the slice of a boat
brushing star grass, lotus, make your wish here,
all this in between-ness swishing around the contours.
There is more invisibility & due to the distance
across rivers, hills, every little thing we've added
the time in between has lengthened like summer.

The Salvation of Words

Brave are the ones whose words of light fell off
cliffs' edges. Caught in mid-air by the hungry
saved in small scraps sewn in dress hems

Sent off in throats. Bergen-Belsen,
Auschwitz-Birkenau. Dark but their skin
turned pale, sallow from months of rank slop.

Void utter dank, fish heads, no pens
captors' shadows stood still
hands poised on gas valves.

Hold close the proof, eye to eye,
prayed words like *forgive them*
All mothers, dads, the innocents came.

Relentless truth delivered riots of words
stained and holy, raged, grand force unstoppable
cuts through fetid fear.

Keep tearing them ripping them from the great liars on high.

There's Something's Happening Here…
—Buffalo Springfield/Stephen Stills

Soon there will be nothing but elephants, small children, egrets,
some falcons, a smattering of poets—no, *legions*, with stars guiding
their hands, elders and shamans
the strong will be riding wild mustangs over bronze hills, calling out
words of praise *all you need is love*, at the top of their lungs.

The learned & chieftains will circle around…say what we crave. Much is already
seeping in, into painters' brushes, in guitars strings and drums' thrum. I hum
the song along with Harrison, Smokey and Dylan, thousands of others.

New flags ripple and wave, anthems are sung in one language—
everyone knows them. Crickets bullfrogs coyotes howl in unison.
Steady flow of rivers, writers, dancers, makers of everything, ALL of
us stay afloat somehow.

It is in the momentum, the sure foot.

Guts

Splayed on sidewalks, alleys and towns where words spit and burn
Throw open the wooden halls hammered and hewn by men
from Haiti, El Salvador, Mexico. Steaming tin shanties.
Stunning, no relief from the heat. Carrion lies still as stone.

Orders from invisible might, muscle under silk suits,
brawny bosses, glint on sunglasses, Secret Service seek the sinners,
scan rooftops, cameras watch, twitch in bushes, wait with rifles.
Presidentes suck money and mint from *mojitos*, slip Berrettas in
leather, dart through gardens, crescendo of palm trees, gardenias,
abandon families, mount women & stallions and ride into nights of
gooseflesh, terror *everywhere*, this happens daily.

Remember that minds shrivel. Songs are lost from souls' repertoires.
Crack things open, silence the growl. Look mercy
in the eye. Mother-of-pearl clouds over you, the delicate village.
Goddesses and demons walk down streets lighting lamps calling
Yes, yes, yes.

What She Left Behind

All dressed up, white cotton gloves, locket & chain, strapless Mary Janes, cat glasses with copper sparkles. Focus, in close, astigmatic, sounding out words: *cumulus, thorough, mambo, determined, pinnacle, alchemy, subrosa* words that invite her to wander and scan a gemmy landscape of the Kingdom of Teen.

Add trappings of boys, joy current of books, Cuba Libras. Fiery petulance swish of dirty blonde hair, laissez-faire. Fillies herself free from the family tether. Natural course of events—training for competition
where only star athletes can be the flailing victors.
Crack the real heart door open.

She lets loose a cry; one she has never heard. No one has ever heard it. Years of masks & folly reveling in long nights too dark to see—
with yips and howls from her feral soul, she hunts for food, her pack. Now she can see through anything. Laser-life.

Over fingers of fog, through olive and pine, above the crows' caw under monarchs' flight, no cover for the past.

Ode to the Labyrinth

Just imagine…blue pills, pink tabs
for all that ails us, the brightest day
the flammability of everything.
How can I sit when all is afire?
Lies, contagious as leprosy—
when was your last encounter with the cure?
Swarms of gnarled words rasp
the same dead message, curl around everyone.
The lucky wrestle their way out.
In shooting stars and sheer cliffs where light,
plant life, grow then burn out and recede,
I see fractions of truth. In a dream, cries
from my thrashing body, find outlined dirt paths
graceful turns—my body rests,
turns to heavy breathing. Sleepwalking
I follow every possibility to find dead ends
then openings. Wordless all we can hear
is the quiet turning,
is it assurance of
 a beginning
and an end?

Aubade

Gossamer fog still covers morning, dear one,
I draw back linen drapes, let light bathe us
before we slip from bliss and peace, you
in your great musculature and I in fragrance called
l'Ombre dans L'Eau. We dove
into each other, complete, with strength of night and days
and now, with energy of constellations
we imbibed last evening, invisible this morning, go—
they are in us. God inside us that echoes,
burns like the shooting star that fell at Eros' feet.
Carry this blessed force of heaven & scent
into the streets, onto autumn drafts,
warm and cool at once, let me know somehow
that this morning will not be the last time
we feel this must and shiver.

A Different America

It starts small, soil from our gardens
seedlings, plants sown with hope
that birds of paradise, daphne and dahlias
will appear. Morning light births brilliance

unachievable any other way.

We till, dig, rake and work it
spread ground cover,
fast-growing. Earth and its dwellers
give off a perfumed energy

wheat, lilies, peonies, corn, ferns, and roses

Mystery of vitamins, presence of weeds, stray paper
bottle caps—clever names on them; Fat Tire
Blue Rock, Dogfish.
Fling seeds, start a wilderness, lead

with thousands of children holding lanterns

they know and, for now, say nothing. They do not need to
Easy smiles, plump cheeks. Keep them in mind.
We will need them. Roughness of trees
brings us to our knees then seeing all there is to know.

Vital information in palm fronds arcing splendor,

Pine trees, mossy lace, cactus blossoms–how
do they ever happen? Pears split, precious amrita flows, marguerites
languish in long grass. All of it. Mother tongue.
These are the ones

in rain & drought—plants, running creatures

great snow drifts, white caps, almighty tornadoes, biblical floods
they find us. Nomadic, maverick flicker in swift moves
announces this odd & rangy americanism. A flavor, a fragrance,
with loud hoots and calls

sever history of ropes that bound many to whipping posts,
boats from old countries over billows of oceans. No more finery
of false lives, arranged marriages, forked tongues.
Banish temples of fear!

Hate, the deafening wind

takes with it everything in its path.
When random terror arrives like fire in massive rage: Dachau
Selma Aleppo Sandy Hook where is the spirit from their light—
low sweet scent of fresh hay, strength of bellows in blacksmiths'
fires,

soul of mustangs running on ancient ranges?

Music, feathered jewelry, prayers, embellishments
there to lead us from gun shots, midden of lives
whose voices were silenced. Small hands of children
clinging to lanterns. They keep coming. Born for that task
and no other.

What lures the haggard from dark houses where no seeds took?

Quiet, like fresh water poised to gush from wells
tapped by sticks, divined by clear voices
from rushing creeks, on hillsides, in nests,
one twig, one blade of dry grass after another.

Vast herds of people

healers, builders, farmers, knitters and painters
who, row after row, pray, nail, plant
knit and mix colors—
another kind of indelible light.

Kat Crawford is a native San Franciscan and currently lives in Tiburon, California, with her husband. She received her Masters' degree in Poetry from Dominican University in 2019. Her work has been published by *Creative Woman, Nomad's Choir, Spillway, Marin Poetry Center Anthology* and *Tuxedo* at Dominican University. She has new poems for the pandemic which will appear in a forthcoming anthology by Diane Frank and Prartho Sereno. Kat's first book in 2014 was *A Particular Heaven*. *All of It* is her first publication of a collection of poetry by a literary press.

www.ingramcontent.com/pod-product-compliance
Lightning Source LLC
LaVergne TN
LVHW040117080426
835507LV00041B/1353